History of
Norse Mythology

www.dinobibi.com

Contents

4

Introduction

Norse mythology is full of stories of powerful gods and goddesses, scary beasts, and lessons on how to live in the tough wilderness the Norse called home. Their beliefs still amaze us today, which is why learning about them is both fun and exciting. You might know the Norse people by a different name: Vikings. You're probably picturing warriors in horned helmets, which isn't completely wrong (aside from the helmets: Vikings never actually wore horned helmets). There was so much more to them, though. Vikings weren't all that good at keeping records, but there's still plenty we know today about who they were, how they lived, and what they believed.

Mythology tells us how people in the past understood the world. They didn't have computers, cell phones, or the Internet to ask questions and find answers. When there was thunder or lightning, they couldn't Google why it happened. They had to come up with their own ideas, which is how every ancient religion started. One question lead to another, then another, and before you know it you had an entire belief system with gods, goddesses, heroes, and villains.

Mythology isn't all just make believe. A lot of the stories the Vikings came up with are based on real life or real events. This method is how historians learn about what life was like a long time ago. They learn the myths and try to figure out if there's any truth behind the legends. Without these stories, we wouldn't know anything about people from the past.

You might wonder why it matters. Why should you read about gods and monsters that aren't real, or learn about people who aren't around anymore? Well, for one, it's cool! Have you heard of the superhero Thor? He's based on a god from Norse mythology. Loki is, too. Vikings may not be around anymore, but their stories are. So are the people who are related to them. Even you might have a Viking ancestor! History is worth learning because it tells us who we used to be. It lets us see what the world was like a long, long time ago. The more you know about the past, the better you understand the present. That's really what history is about—understanding.

It's time to learn more about the amazing people who lived over 1,000 years ago and came up with amazing stories that still interest us to this day. Welcome to the world of Norse mythology.

Chapter 1:
Who Were the Norsemen
(Norse People)?

Before we talk about mythology, let's look at who exactly the Norse people were. Where did they live? What did they do all day? What language did they speak? All these things tell us more about Norse culture in general and help some of the weirder stories in Norse mythology make sense.

Norse vs Vikings

First, let's talk about the difference between the Norsemen and Vikings and how they're related. Basically, Vikings were a smaller group of Norse people who were warriors and went off to sea. They're more famous than the farmers and everyday Norse people who stayed behind on land, but at the end of the day they were the same. When you read about Norse mythology, you'll often see the name "Vikings" instead of "Norse" because Vikings are usually who we are most interested in. The period when the Norsemen lived is even known as the "Viking Age."

In this book we will use the terms Norsemen, Norse people, and Vikings. Just remember that they're the same people from the same place and time.

Where and When Did They Live?

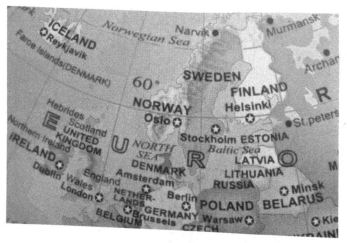

Map of Scandanavia

The Viking Age, which is the period that the Norse lived in, lasted from 793-1066 CE (Common Era). This was around the same time as the Middle Ages in Europe, which started in 476 CE and ended in 1492. These two ages go by different names because "Viking Age" refers to Scandinavian history, while "Middle Ages" covers the rest of Europe.

Scandinavia is a vast area that we know today as Norway, Denmark, and Sweden. If you look at a map, you'll find these three countries above Germany, France, and the United Kingdom, and to the left of Russia. This tells you a lot about what the weather was like—cold.

What Was Life Like for Them?

While Vikings lived an exciting and dangerous life of exploring, sailing, and raiding, most Norse people were farmers. Back then, if you wanted to eat, you had to grow or raise your food yourself. Since many Norse villages were near the ocean, fishing was just as important as farming.

Dried fish

Remember that where they lived, winter could get very cold. An early winter could kill crops, and a cold spring could stop them from growing anything. This weather made life harder for them than it might have been for other groups in warmer places.

Norse people lived on farmsteads in villages, small hamlets, or sometimes even alone in the forest or mountains. Villages could have up to fifty farmsteads, while hamlets usually had four or fewer. On these farmsteads, families raised crops and animals, made clothes, and did their best to survive.

Village in Viking farm at Norway

Life wasn't easy, and a lot of people got sick or starved. The Norse were tough, though. That's part of the reason we know so much about Vikings, who might have been the toughest of them all. Long before Christopher Columbus sailed to North America, the Vikings made it there and even as far as Baghdad in Eastern Europe. All this traveling (and stealing along the way) meant they ran into many different groups of people. Wherever they went, stories were written about them, and a lot of these stories still exist.

How Do We Know Anything about Norse Mythology?

If the Norse people lived so long ago, how do we know anything about them? The way we learn about the past today is by reading books written a long time ago. We can also learn about other cultures through archeology. Archeology means to study humans who lived before we did. We can find out about them by digging around places that used to be their homes. Sometimes we find pottery, jewelry, and even tools they made. These old objects are called artifacts.

Books and artifacts from the Viking Age tell us a lot about how the Norse people lived. We've found 1,000-year-old swords, rune stones, and a lot of amulets with pictures of the gods on them. We have even found entire Viking ships!

Norse ship

There are two main books that tell us a lot about Norse mythology. These books are the *Poetic Edda* and the *Prose Edda*. An edda is a book written in the Old Norse language. Both books were written a long time after the Viking Age, but they still hold a lot of information.

The Poetic Edda

Just like the name says, the *Poetic Edda* is a book of poems that are all about Norse mythology. Most of the information in the *Poetic Edda* comes from two poems: "Völuspá", which means "The Insight of the Seeress," and "Grímnismál", which means "The Song of the Hooded One." Before these stories were written down, they were passed down orally. This means that people remembered the stories and told them to each other for years and years.

The poem with the most information about Norse mythology is "Völuspá". In this poem, Odin, the leader of the gods, goes to a wise woman and asks her to tell the future. To prove that she really does know what's going to happen, he asks her to tell him about the past. She doesn't know anything about Odin, but she is still able to tell him how the cosmos, in other words the universe, was made (which you will learn about in the next chapter) and where the first dwarves, elves, and humans came from. She was also able to tell Odin some things that only he could know. This proved that she really was a wise woman, so Odin had her tell him about the future. In the future, she could see the end of the world and how all

Norse Language

The Norse of Scandinavia spoke a language called Old Norse. They wrote in an alphabet that used runes, which are symbols that stand for letters and ideas. There were two alphabets, one from before the Viking Age, Elder Futhark consisting of 24 letters, and the other, Younger Futhark, at the beginning of the Viking Age.

Elder Futhark.

Here is what the first six runes look like and what they mean:

- ᚠ: "Fehu" means wealth (literally translates to "cattle," because in the Viking Age if you had more cattle, or cows, you had more money).

- ᚢ: "Uruz" means strength of will (like willpower).
- ᚦ: "Thurisaz" means giant and danger.
- ᚨ: "Ansuz" means an Aesir god, like Odin.
- ᚱ: "Raidho" means journey on horseback or moving.
- ᚲ: "Kaunan" means ulcer and pain. An ulcer is a kind of sore spot in your body that's on the inside.

The second, Younger Futhark, was used for poems, official documents, and everyday writing. You'll learn more about the runes later when we talk about the god Odin, who, according to legend, was the one who discovered the runes.

Younger Futhark

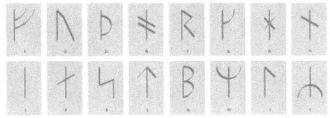

Set of monochrome icons with Younger Futhark.

The first six runes spell out "futhark," which is why the Norse alphabets are called the Elder Futhark and the Younger Futhark.

Rune stone

What Happened to the Vikings?

Technically, nothing happened to the Vikings. They didn't die off or disappear. They spread out around the world, changed their religion, and then stopped raiding.

They became Icelanders, Norwegians, Greenlanders, Swedes, and Danes, depending on where they lived. In fact, a lot of people who live in Iceland (Icelanders) are descendants of Vikings! In the end, the names "Norsemen" and "Vikings" disappeared rather than the people.

How Do We Know Anything about Norse Mythology?

If the Norse people lived so long ago, how do we know anything about them? The way we learn about the past today is by reading books written a long time ago. We can also learn about other cultures through archeology. Archeology means to study humans who lived before we did. We can find out about them by digging around places that used to be their homes. Sometimes we find pottery, jewelry, and even tools they made. These old objects are called artifacts.

Books and artifacts from the Viking Age tell us a lot about how the Norse people lived. We've found 1,000-year-old swords, rune stones, and a lot of amulets with pictures of the gods on them. We have even found entire Viking ships!

Norse ship

There are two main books that tell us a lot about Norse mythology. These books are the *Poetic Edda* and the *Prose Edda*. An edda is a book written in the Old Norse language. Both books were written a long time after the Viking Age, but they still hold a lot of information.

The Poetic Edda

Just like the name says, the *Poetic Edda* is a book of poems that are all about Norse mythology. Most of the information in the *Poetic Edda* comes from two poems: "Völuspá", which means "The Insight of the Seeress," and "Grímnismál", which means "The Song of the Hooded One." Before these stories were written down, they were passed down orally. This means that people remembered the stories and told them to each other for years and years.

The poem with the most information about Norse mythology is "Völuspá". In this poem, Odin, the leader of the gods, goes to a wise woman and asks her to tell the future. To prove that she really does know what's going to happen, he asks her to tell him about the past. She doesn't know anything about Odin, but she is still able to tell him how the cosmos, in other words the universe, was made (which you will learn about in the next chapter) and where the first dwarves, elves, and humans came from. She was also able to tell Odin some things that only he could know. This proved that she really was a wise woman, so Odin had her tell him about the future. In the future, she could see the end of the world and how all the gods would die. We will talk about the end of the gods in Chapter 6.

The *Poetic Edda* isn't easy for us to understand nowadays, but in the past, when people still believed in the Norse gods, it made perfect sense.

The Prose Edda

Snorri Sturluson, an Icelandic scholar, wrote The *Prose Edda*. A scholar is someone who knows a lot about a subject. Snorri knew a lot about Norse history and mythology. His book has a lot of the same poems and information as the *Poetic Edda*. He also added a lot of new information. Some of the poems in the *Prose Edda* are copied from older poems that don't exist anymore. Not all the things Snorri wrote down are true. He did make up some things and change the stories a little bit. Something you should always remember about some books is that not everything you read is true. People can write down anything they want, and sometimes what they write down isn't what really happened. Luckily, we know which parts of the stories Snorri made up. In this book, we tell the stories that Snorri didn't change.

The very first story you will learn, which comes from the *Poetic Edda*, is the Norse story about how the world started. In mythology, stories about the beginning of the world are called creation stories, or creation myths.

Chapter 2:
The Norse Story of Creation

Every mythology has a creation story that explains how the world started. Today, we know that the universe started with the Big Bang. Before we knew this, though, we had to come up with our own ideas about what happened. Creation stories can tell you a lot about the people who invented them. They're usually based on where the people lived, what their lives were like, and what they thought was the meaning of life.

Most creation stories start with nothing. Can you picture nothing? No sky, no ground, no trees, or cars, or people. Not a single thing existed in the very beginning. Then something happened, and that something is the first piece of Norse mythology.

The Beginning of the Cosmos

Norse mythology starts with how the cosmos, the universe and everything in it, was made. It's basically everything that ever was or will be. Without a cosmos, you can't have anything else.

The Norse believed that at the very beginning of time, there were just three worlds:

- Muspelheim, made of fire

- Niflheim, made of ice
- Ginnungagap, a bottomless pit of darkness

Ginnungagap was in between Muspelheim and Niflheim. These two worlds of fire and ice shot out frost and flames, which would sometimes hit each other and fall into Ginnungagap. The drips of melted ice stuck together to make the giant, Ymir. Other giants split off from Ymir's body, the way cells in your body split apart to form new cells.

How the First Gods Were Born

Ymir and the giants weren't alone. The melted ice that made Ymir also made a cow, Audhumla, who ate a salt-lick that came from the ice that was still dripping. When she got to the bottom of the salt-lick, there was a person! This person was named Buri, the very first Aesir, which is a tribe of gods.

Buri had a son named Borr (sometimes spelled Bor), who married the daughter of one of the giants that came from Ymir. Borr and his wife, Bestla, were the parents of Odin. Since Borr was almost a god and Bestla was a giant, Odin was half-god and half-giant. This made him fit to be the chief of the Aesir tribe.

Odin also had two brothers, Vili and Ve. Together, the three of them made the rest of the world, including the sky, land, plants, oceans, and clouds.

Making a World

The story of how the world was made is a little dark. Most creation myths use the body of a god or some other type of creature to make the Earth. The Norse story of creation does the same thing.

Ymir was still around after Odin and his brothers were born, but he wasn't a nice guy. In fact, Ymir had turned so evil that Odin, Vili, and Ve had to kill him. Using Ymir's body, they made everything. His skull made the sky, his skin became soil and dirt, his hair turned into plants, and the oceans came from his blood.

After they made the world, the three gods decided it was time to fill it with a new race of creatures. Using two tree trunks, they made the first humans, Ask and Embla. The gods put humans in the "human world," known as Midgard. They also put up a fence around Midgard so the giants, who lived in Jotunheim, wouldn't be able to hurt the humans.

The creation story ends when humans are made. The great myths come after that! Before you learn any of these, though, you need to know about the other worlds besides Midgard, Jotunheim, Muspelheim, and Niflheim.

There are a lot of worlds in Norse mythology—nine, to be exact! You'll learn all about these worlds in the next chapter.

Chapter 3:
Yggdrasil and the Nine Worlds

Yggdrasil

You just learned how the Norse believed the cosmos was made, but do you know where they thought the cosmos was?

What we think of the cosmos today is all around us. It's not really shaped like anything, and it exists in every direction as far as we can see. To the Norse, though, the cosmos was shaped like a giant tree that held all nine of their worlds. These nine worlds were all on different parts of the tree, from the trunk all the way up to the top branches. We don't know exactly where on the tree every world was supposed to be, but we can guess.

The name of this great world tree is Yggdrasil, which means "Horse of Odin."

The Nine Worlds

Nine Worlds

over them, and what better place to see the Earth than from above?

While most of the worlds are separated from each other, Asgard and Midgard (the world of humans) are connected by the Bifrost bridge. The Bifrost is a rainbow bridge that's always guarded to keep both Asgard and Midgard safe.

The Norse believed that each god had his own palace in Asgard and that the city of the Aesir was also divided into 12 other realms. One of these realms was Valhalla, which was basically Heaven for Vikings. Vikings wanted to go there when they died, but they believed they were only allowed in Valhalla if they died heroically or in battle.

Midgard

Midgard is Earth. You're in Midgard right now. The name means "Middle Enclosure," which is what the Norse saw their world as. Remember that Odin and his brothers made the first humans, then put a fence around Midgard to keep the humans safe. Even though the Norse thought of the Earth as a kind of enclosure, they explored it far and wide.

Vanaheim

Vanaheim is the home of the other tribe of gods, the Vanir. The Vanir were more like nature gods, while the Aesir were mostly gods of war and power. Not much written about Vanaheim or the Vanir is still around. All we really know about them is that they were just a little bit different from the Aesir, but the Norse people still saw them as gods.

Jotunheim

Jotunheim is the wild world of the giants. It surrounds Midgard, the human world, but is separated by the fence set up by Odin and his brothers.

The Norse thought the giants were wild and untamed. They probably weren't too happy about Odin killing Ymir. Giants had powers just like the Vanir and Aesir gods. That's why Odin wanted to protect the human world from them.

In the Old Norse language, giants were called jötnar. Jötnar means "devourer," and that name describes them perfectly. The giants wanted to tear down cities like Asgard and make the world wild and chaotic. The Asgardians wanted the world to be safe and orderly. Therefore, the giants of Jotunheim and the gods of Asgard were opposites and enemies.

Niflheim

If you remember from the creation story in Chapter 2, Niflheim is the ice world. The name Niflheim means "World of Fog." It is dark, cold, and filled with mist and ice. Since much of the land the Norse people lived on was the same way, it makes sense that they would have an entire world in their mythology made of ice!

Muspelheim

Muspelheim is the other world from the creation story. Instead of ice, though, Muspelheim is filled with fire. Surt, the fire giant, lives in Muspelheim. Viking legends said that Surt would use fire from Muspelheim to end the world during Ragnarök.

Alfheim

No mythology would be complete without elves! Alfheim means "Homeland of the Elves." These beings were supposed to be more beautiful than anyone or anything. One of the Vanir gods, Freyr, rules Alfheim. The Vanir and the elves are probably related, but the Norse never described how.

Nidavellir

You might also see Nidavellir called Svartalfheim, which means "Homeland of the Black Elves." "Black elves" is another name for dwarves, who were the ones living in Nidavellir. Dwarves were craftsmen who lived underground and mined for gems. They made a lot of amazing weapons including Thor's famous hammer, Odin's spear, and many other things like ships and jewelry.

Hel

The name might sound scary, but Hel, or Helheim, isn't that bad. It's the Norse underworld where people went after they died if they weren't warriors. Life almost continued like normal in Hel. The people there could still eat, drink, and sleep. They just weren't in Midgard anymore, so they couldn't see or talk to anybody who wasn't in Hel. Sometimes, gods or other people who were still alive could go to Hel to talk to the dead or bring someone back to life. They got to Hel by following the road there, called Helvegr.

Chapter 4:
Norse Gods and Goddesses

Ancient Norse Mythology Gods and Goddesses Characters Icon Set

It's time to look at the main characters in every mythology—
the gods and goddesses! There are several goddesses and even
more gods. We don't know about every single one of them

because there were just too many to keep track of. We do know about the most important ones, though.

The gods and goddesses are divided into two tribes: the Aesir and the Vanir. While both tribes are similar, they don't always agree, which is why they live in different worlds. There are more Aesir gods and goddesses than Vanir, but that might just be because we don't know about the other Vanir.

While a lot of religions believe in one god (a "supreme being"), the Norse thought that all the gods and goddesses shared power. No one god ruled over everybody else, and everyone had a job to do. Some gods helped warriors, and a few goddesses took care of mothers and children. All the gods and goddesses had one main job, though. They were all supposed to protect humans from the giants who wanted to destroy everything.

There are so many stories about the gods, but talking about all of them would take up another book! Instead, you'll just learn about some of the most important things that each god and goddess is known for.

Aesir Gods

Odin

Odin

Odin is by far the most important god in Norse mythology. He was around almost from the beginning, helped create the cosmos, and ruled Asgard. Odin is known as a god of war, magic, wisdom, and even poetry. He was terrifying on the battlefield, making him a great warrior. At the same time, he only ever spoke in poems. These poems were so beautiful that others couldn't help but listen to him.

Odin only had one eye, and the story of how he lost his other eye is famous. One thing Odin wanted more than anything else is wisdom. Wisdom basically means knowing a lot, and Odin wanted to know everything. In Norse mythology, if you wanted wisdom, you had to go to the Well of Urd, also called Mimir's Well, because it was the home of a being called Mimir. The water of Mimir's Well held all the knowledge in the cosmos, so Odin went there to ask for a drink so he could know more, too.

Mimir couldn't just give the water away, since knowledge is very valuable. He asked Odin for an eye in return for a drink of water. You can probably guess what happened next. Since what he wanted was wisdom, Odin gladly gave over an eye and then drank from the well. No one knows exactly what he learned when he drank the water, though.

An eye wasn't the only thing Odin gave up in exchange for knowledge. Another story tells of him hanging himself from Yggdrasil for nine days and nights to learn about the runes. These runes are the same ones that the Norse people used as their alphabet. Remember that the runes are both letters and symbols of ideas. So, Odin wasn't just trying to learn the alphabet. He wanted to know what the runes looked like and meant because their symbols contained magic.

The wisdom Odin got from both the well and the runes made him one of the wisest and most powerful gods. His knowledge is one of the reasons why another name he went by was "Allfather." He had the power to give life or take it away, and a lot of the time he did both.

Odin

Vili and Ve

Also mentioned in Chapter 2, Vili and Ve are the brothers of Odin, and they helped him create the world. There aren't many stories about Vili and Ve after the creation of the cosmos.

Vili's name means "will," and he is sometimes called the god of motivation. When Vili, Ve, and Odin made the first humans, Vili game them the ability to think and feel.

Ve's name means "temple." He is the god of the sacred, which means anything that has to do with the gods. After Vili gave the first humans the gifts of thinking and feeling, Ve gave them speech, sight, and hearing.

Thor

Everyone knows about the superhero Thor, but the Norse god Thor is a little bit different. He is the son of Odin and Jord, who was a giant. This makes Thor a giant too, since his father is half-giant.

Thor is the god of thunder. He is the perfect example of an idea warrior. Every Viking looked up to Thor. He is courageous, strong, and a loyal defender of Asgard.

While Thor also had a belt that gave him strength, his most famous possession is his hammer, Mjöllnir, which means "lightning." The lightning hammer used by the thunder god is one way the Norse explained thunderstorms. When you hear thunder and see lightning, it's Thor riding on a chariot in the sky, slaying giants.

Since Thor is the god of thunder, he also has some power over rain. The Norse believed he could help their crops grow by controlling the weather.

Mjöllnir

Thor and his hammer were both very important symbols later in the Viking Age. Other people who came to Scandinavia to try to change the religion of the Norse brought amulets shaped like crosses. These crosses symbolized Christianity. The Norse, instead of wearing the cross amulets, started wearing necklaces with the symbol of Thor's hammer on them. They had believed in Thor and the other gods for a very long time, and these necklaces showed that they were going to keep right on believing.

Necklace of Thor's hammer

Baldur

Baldur

Baldur is the son of Odin and Frigg. He is the god of light, sun, and joy. He makes everyone happy and shines with light that comes from his skin.

The main story about Baldur is how he died. He started dreaming about his death, which scared his mother, Frigg. She asked everything that existed to promise not to hurt Baldur. She asked weapons like spears and axes, and even plants like trees and flowers. The one thing she didn't ask not to hurt her son was mistletoe.

Loki, the mischievous god, convinced another god to throw mistletoe at Baldur, because nothing else could hurt him. The mistletoe killed Baldur, and he went to the underworld, Hel.

One of Baldur's brothers took Helvegr, the road to Hel, to try to get his brother back. He couldn't, so Baldur stayed in the underworld forever.

Loki

Loki

Loki is famously known as the trickster god. While most of the other gods like and take care of each other, Loki is the outcast. He goes back and forth between helping the gods and helping the giants. He can be playful and funny, but most of the time he's not a nice guy. In many of the stories about Loki, his tricks get him into trouble. One of these stories is about the making of Thor's hammer.

Thor had a wife named Sif. She had beautiful, long golden hair. One day when Loki was bored, he decided to cut off Sif's hair. Thor was very mad and threatened to beat up Loki. To stop Thor from hurting him, Loki promised to have a new head of hair made for Sif. He went to Nidavellir, the home of the dwarves, to have the head of hair made. Dwarves were the best craftsmen, and they were able to make new hair for Sif. They also made a ship named Skidbladnir that could fold up to the size of a pocket and a mighty spear called Gungnir.

Loki could have gone back to Asgard with the ship, spear, and hair, but he wanted to play another trick. He dared two dwarf brothers, Brokkr and Sindri, to make three more things that were even better than Sif's hair, Skidbladnir, and Gungnir. He promised that if they did, they could have his head.

Brokkr and Sindri worked and worked, and while they did, Loki, disguised as a fly, tried to bite them to make them mess up. They were able to make three more amazing things even with Loki's mischief. These gifts included a boar (a pig with tusks) named Gullinbursti that gave off light and could run on land, in water, and in the air. There was also a gold ring named Draupnir that could make more rings, and, best of all, the hammer, Mjöllnir. All these creations were perfect, except Mjöllnir, which had a handle that was too short. Thor was happy with it anyway, and the other gifts went to Odin (the ring and the spear) and Freyr (the ship and the boar).

There was still one problem, though. The three gifts Brokkr and Sindri made were better than the first three, so Loki owed them his head. When they went to cut it off, he reminded them that he promised his head and not his neck. So, since Loki had bitten them when he was a fly, Brokkr and Sindri sewed his mouth shut instead of taking his head.

Heimdall

Remember how the Bifrost Bridge connecting Asgard and Midgard is always guarded? Well, Heimdall, another one of Odin's sons, is the guardian. His home is on top of the Bifrost so he is always there to watch over it. He almost never sleeps, he can see as well as a bird can, and he can hear very well, too. Heimdall holds the horn called Gjallarhorn, which he only uses to let the gods of Asgard know when there are intruders.

Tyr

Tyr

Tyr is the ultimate war god. He was very important to the Norse people, who valued strength in battle, law, and justice. Try represents all these things. Vikings would often ask Tyr for strength in battle and to help them achieve victory.

Tyr didn't just symbolize war, though. He believed in fairness and justice. He was almost like the judge and jury of the Norse gods. There's one story with Tyr that shows just how much he cared about his fellow gods.

One of the most famous and terrifying creatures from Norse mythology is Fenrir the wolf. Fenrir was one of Loki's children. All the gods were afraid of Fenrir because of how strong and scary he was. They decided that it would be safer to lock him up, but he broke out of every chain they put him in. Finally, they had the dwarves make an unbreakable chain. Fenrir thought they were testing his strength, but the chain looked weak to him. Fenrir thought the gods might be tricking him, so he asked for one of the gods to put his arm in his (Fenrir's) mouth to prove that they weren't. Tyr was the only god who was brave enough to stick his hand in the wolf's mouth. When they wrapped Fenrir in the chain made by the dwarves, he was finally trapped. Fenrir was so mad that he bit Tyr's hand off.

Fenrir

The point of this story is that Tyr knew he was in danger, but he also knew that giving his hand to the wolf was the only way to protect everyone else.

Mani

Moon chariot

Mani means "moon," which this god represents. He has a sister, Sol, who is the goddess of the sun. When the cosmos was first created, Mani didn't know that his job was to bring out the moon every night. Later, the gods created the phases of the moon so that Mani would know where he had to be every night. He pulls the moon across the sky using a horse drawn chariot, just like his sister does for the sun. You'll learn more about Mani's sister later.

Ullr

Not a lot of information exists about Ullr, but what we do know is that he was very important to the Norse. He was an expert hunter and archer who took Odin's place as chief of the Aesir when Odin was gone at one point.

There are a lot of places in Norway and Sweden that have "ullr" in their name. This proves that, in the Viking Age, Ullr was an important god. Sadly, this is all we know about him.

Aesir Goddesses

Frigg

Frigg

Frigg is Odin's wife and the highest-ranking goddess is Asgard. She practices a type of magic called seidr, which involves learning about the future and changing it, if possible. Some Norse women practice seidr, and they would sometimes perform magic in exchange for food or a place to sleep. Frigg's name means "beloved" and she represents love and marriage.

Sigyn

Sigyn is Loki's wife. There aren't a lot of stories about her, but there is one that shows how much she loved Loki.

After Loki convinced one of the other gods to kill Baldur (accidentally), the rest of the gods punished him. They tied him down in a cave and put a snake that dripped venom over him. To stop the venom from hitting Loki, Sigyn sat next to him with a bowl to catch the venom.

Idun

Idun

Idun is the goddess that carries the fruits of immortality that let the gods stay young and live (almost) forever. The best-known story about Idun is one where she is kidnapped thanks to Loki.

Loki got into a fight with a giant disguised as an eagle. The eagle eventually grabbed Loki and started to fly away with him. Loki wanted the eagle to put him back on the ground, but the eagle said he wouldn't do it unless Loki brought the goddess Idun to him. What the eagle really wanted was the fruit of immortality. To save himself, Loki said he would bring Idun.

Loki tricked Idun into leaving Asgard by telling her there were fruits better than hers outside the city's walls. When she left the safety of Asgard, the eagle took her.

Without Idun and the immortality fruits, the gods started to get old. They figured out it was Loki's fault that Idun was missing, so they threatened to kill him if he didn't bring her back. Again, to save his own skin, Loki went to the land of the giants and rescued Idun. The giant who had taken her, still disguised as an eagle, chased after Loki, but the other gods were able to defeat him.

Sif

You might remember Sif from the story about Thor's hammer. She is Thor's wife, and might be the mother of Ullr. Her long golden hair is symbolic of fields of grain, which were very important to the Norse. Since Thor's powers are related to storms and rain, their marriage makes sense. Together, Sif and Thor represent harvest, the time when the Norse could stock up on food. There was even a plant with a name that means "Sif's hair" in Old Norse. That tells you just how much the Norse loved Sif!

Sol

Sun chariot

Sol is the sister of Mani, the god of the moon. Sol is the goddess of the sun and pulls it across the sky every day with a horse-drawn chariot. Her horses are Árvakr, which means early riser, and Alsviðr, which means swift. Alsviðr and Árvakr are very fast because they're chased across the sky by wolves every day.

Gefjun

The Gefion Fountain in Copenhagen, Denmark, designed by Danish artist Anders Bundgaard 1908, and is attributed to Prose Edda.

Gefjun's (or Gefion) name means "giver" or "generous one," which is exactly who she is. She is the goddess of abundance and agriculture. Most of the stories with Gefjun talk about her helping farmers and making sure the land is ready to grow crops.

Vanir Gods

Odr

Nothing is known about Odr other than that he is just like Odin, but he rules the Vanir instead of the Aesir. He also has a daughter named Hnoss.

Freyr

Freyr

Freyr might be a Vanir god, but he is supposedly good friends with the Aesir tribe, too. He was a very well-loved god to the

Norse people. Freyr brings wealth, peace, good health, and good harvests.

Freyr lives in Alfheim with the elves instead of in Vanir with the other gods of his tribe. When Loki brought back Thor's hammer along with all the other gifts from the dwarves, Freyr received the ship Skidbladnir and the boar Gullinbursti.

Njord

Njord

Njord is the father of Freyr and Freya. He is the god of the sea and was a favorite among the Vikings who set sail to new lands. Njord also represents wealth and money. Norse people who were rich were said to be "as rich as Njord."

Vanir Goddesses

Freya

Freya among the dwarves

Freya is the wife of Odr. Since Odr is the Odin of the Vanir tribe, Freya is the Frigg of the Vanir. She represents love and beauty. Like Frigg, Freya practices seidr magic.

Nerthus

Nerthus is Njord's sister and represents Mother Earth. She is a goddess who likes peace, and the people who worshipped her would lock up all their weapons for a few days when they thought she would visit their homes or villages. Besides her love of non-violence, nothing else is really known about Nerthus.

The Aesir-Vanir War

Gods and goddesses don't always get along. In Norse mythology, it wasn't just Loki who caused trouble. The Aesir and Vanir tribes had one big fight that turned into a war.

The war started when Freya, a Vanir goddess, decided to leave Vanaheim and wander around the worlds of Yggdrasil. If you remember, Freya practiced seidr magic. This practice made her popular in the other worlds, because magic could be very helpful. After going to many different worlds, Freya ended up in Asgard. She used a different name, though, so the other gods wouldn't know who she was.

Freya was very powerful, and all the Aesir gods in Asgard wanted her to use magic for them. They started fighting over who would get to ask her for help first. They finally realized they were being selfish. In Asgard, being selfish was a very bad thing. The gods and goddesses were supposed to think of each other first. They blamed Freya for making them selfish and tried to punish her. Even though they tried to kill her three times, Freya didn't die. She went back to Vanaheim and told the other Vanir gods and goddesses what the Aesir tribe tried to do to her. This treatment made the Vanir mad.

The Aesir were afraid of the Vanir and the powers the tribe had, and the Vanir didn't like the Aesir because they had tried to hurt Freya. Both tribes eventually were so mad at each other that they started to fight. The Aesir used regular weapons to fight, and the Vanir used magic. Since both tribes consisted of powerful gods and goddesses, there was no winner. They just kept fighting.

After a very long time, the Aesir and Vanir were tired of the war. All the gods and goddesses agreed to stop fighting. They called a truce then traded hostages. This act was something that the Norse did, too. Whenever two sides would stop fighting, they would give each other people from their tribe. This was called "paying tribute."

The Vanir gave the Aesir Freya, Freyr, and Njord. The Aesir gave the Vanir Hoenir and Mimir. We didn't talk about Hoenir or Mimir when we listed the Aesir gods, because we don't know a lot about them. Hoenir might have been a god, but he wasn't very smart. Mimir was an advisor to the gods, which means he gave them advice. Mimir was very wise, but we don't know if he was a god too or a giant.

The reason the Aesir gave the Vanir Hoenir, who wasn't smart, and Mimir, who was smart, is because Hoenir could be smart too, but only if Mimir was around. Whenever Mimir was away from Hoenir, he gave bad advice. After he gave the Vanir gods bad advice too many times, they sent him back to Asgard. The Vanir thought the Aesir had sent them a dumb god on purpose, so they cut off Mimir's head and sent that to Asgard, too. Odin was able to save Mimir's head and keep Mimir alive. Mimir (actually Mimir's head) became Odin's advisor.

The war almost started again because of what the Vanir did, but both tribes realized it would be stupid to keep fighting. Instead, every single god and goddess from both Vanir and Aesir spat into a cauldron. The spit mixed together and made a new god named Kvasir.

Kvasir was the wisest of all beings. He was even wiser than Odin, which is saying something. Kvasir wandered around the different worlds and gave advice to anyone who asked.

ODIN   THOR   FREYA   LOKI

FREYR   FRIGG   BALDER   TYR

Norse Germanic gods mythology

Chapter 5:
Creatures of Norse Mythology

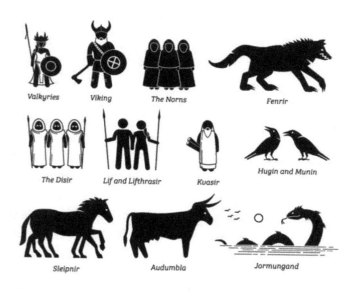

Valkyries   Viking   The Norns   Fenrir

The Disir   Lif and Lifthrasir   Kvasir   Hugin and Munin

Sleipnir   Audumbla   Jormungand

Ancient Norse Mythology People, Monsters and Creatures Characters Icon Set

Gods and goddesses aren't the only important characters in Norse mythology. A lot of the legends and stories are about fights the gods have with different creatures. You've already met some of these creatures, like Fenrir, but others will be new. This chapter also talks more about the elves and dwarves who live in their own worlds and don't spend much time with the gods.

Fenrir

Fenrir, the wolf who bit off Tyr's hand, is one of the scariest beasts in Norse mythology. Even the gods were afraid of him. Fenrir is Loki's son, which might seem weird since he's an animal. Gods could do that, though. Most of Loki's children were animals, not people.

Even when Fenrir was a baby wolf, the Aesir gods knew he would be very powerful. Since he was Loki's son, they were afraid he would be trouble just like Loki. They raised Fenrir in Asgard so they could keep an eye on him. It's a good thing they did, because he grew very fast. The gods realized that to control him, they would have to chain him up before he got too big. You probably remember what happened from the last chapter. Tyr put his hand in Fenrir's mouth so the gods could chain him up, and Fenrir bit Tyr's hand off. They tied Fenrir's chain to a boulder, and the gods put a sword in his mouth so he couldn't bite anyone else. Fenrir was so mad that he howled and howled, and all that howling made him drool. The drool formed a river that the Norse called "Expectation."

Fenrir wasn't stuck to the boulder forever, though. He gets revenge in Ragnarök, which you'll learn about in the next chapter.

Jormungand

Jormungand

Jormungand means "Great Beast," and that's exactly what he is. He's a serpent (a giant snake) that is so big, his entire body surrounds Midgard. Jormungand is another one of Loki's sons. Just like Fenrir, the gods don't really like him. Out of all the gods, Thor hates Jormungand the most. They fought twice, and the last time was in Ragnarök. To find out what happened, don't skip Chapter 6!

In their first battle, Thor was fishing with a giant named Hymir. Jormungand lives in the ocean between Asgard and Midgard, and Thor wanted to catch him. He almost did, too. Thor caught Jormungand on his fishing line, and Thor was reeling him in. Hymir the giant was afraid of Jormungand, so he cut the fishing line and let the serpent go. Thor was so mad, he threw Hymir overboard.

Nidhogg

Nidhogg is another serpent, but he lives under Yggdrasil. He eats the roots of the world tree which is very bad for the tree. The Norse believed he was a kind of giant who was trying to destroy the cosmos and everything in it. During Ragnarök, Nidhogg left his spot under Yggdrasil to help the giants. You'll learn about this in the next chapter.

Sleipnir

Sleipnir

Sleipnir is Odin's horse. Sleipnir has eight legs and helps Odin get around to the different worlds of Yggdrasil. Sleipnir is another one of Loki's sons, but the gods aren't afraid of him. Out of all the horses in Asgard, Sleipnir is the best.

Hugin and Munin

Hugin and Munin

Odin has two ravens that help him in battle and bring him messages. These ravens are Hugin and Munin. Since Odin is one of the gods of war and battles, and ravens usually hang around battles, Odin is sometimes called the "raven god." The Norse thought ravens were either Odin in disguise or Odin's messengers. Hugin and Munin fly around Yggdrasil, listening to everyone and finding out news to bring back to Odin. Ravens are very smart birds, which is why Odin uses them.

Berserkers and Úlfheðnar

The Norse people thought that they could learn a lot from nature. They had shamans, which are people who believe they can connect to the spirit world or change their shape and become the spirit of an animal. Berserkers were shamans that became bear spirits on the battlefield. They wanted to be as strong and fierce as bears, so they wore bear skins and roared. There were also úlfheðnar (oolv-HETH-nahr), which are shamans who become wolf spirits instead of bear spirits. These shamans wore wolf pelts and howled at their enemies.

Berserkers and úlfheðnar were also called "Odin's men" because Odin gave them their powers and ability to change shape.

Norns

Everyone is afraid of the Norns, even the gods. The Norns control fate, which is what happens in the future. They can change it whenever they want to, and there is nothing anyone can do about it.

The Norns are three women who live underneath Yggdrasil. Their home is near the Well of Fate. The names of the Norns are Urd, which means "the past," Verdandi, which means "the present," and Skuld, "the future." They are not gods, elves, dwarves, or any other type of being from Norse mythology. The Norns seem almost like humans, but they're not. They're a lot more powerful. Even the gods can't control fate, so the Norns had the ability to do what even Odin couldn't do.

Whenever something happened in the life of a Viking they weren't happy with, they blamed the Norns. No one ever asked the Norns to change his or her fate, though. The Norse people knew they had to be okay with whatever the Norns decided to do with their future.

Elves

Elves

Elves are almost gods, but not exactly. They live in Alfheim, which is a beautiful land ruled by the Vanir god, Freyr.

Elves are known for their beauty and magic powers. They can either heal humans or make them sick, and they like to do both. They aren't interested in anything that happens in the other nine worlds. Some elves marry humans, so their kids are half elf and half human. The human children of elves have magic powers that other humans don't have. Sometimes, when a human dies, he or she goes to Alfheim and becomes an elf instead of going to Hel or Valhalla.

Elves were kind of like perfect versions of humans to the Norse people, which is one reason they worshipped them.

Dwarves

We usually think of dwarves as short, fat, bearded men. The Norse didn't think of them this way, though. The reason dwarves are called "black elves" is because they are like the elves, only they are pitch black because they live underground. Their home is in Nidavellir, which is full of mines and tunnels where they dig for metals and gems to craft with. Dwarves love making things, and they're very good at it. In a lot of Norse stories, dwarves are the ones who make objects for the gods, like Fenrir's unbreakable chain and Thor's hammer. They also made things like Odin's spear, Sif's hair, Freya's necklace, and a magic ring.

Dwarves were even around during the creation of the cosmos. When Odin and his brothers used Ymir's body to make the world, they asked four dwarves to help hold up the sky. These dwarves are Austri, Vestri, Nordri, and Sudri. Each dwarf holds a different part of the sky. Austri holds the east, Vestri the west, Nordri is in the north, and Sudri is the south.

Valkyries

Valkyrie and Valhalla

The name Valkyrie means "choosers of the fallen." Valkyries are Odin's helpers. They are female spirits who collect the spirits of warriors and take them to Valhalla. They don't take every warrior, though. Odin tells the Valkyries which warriors he wants in his home. These warriors will eventually help Odin during Ragnarök.

Valkyries don't just take warriors who have died to Valhalla. On the battlefield, they also get to decide who lives and who dies. They're a little bit like the Norns, but they only have control over the fate of warriors, not everyone else.

There are a few more creatures and beings that the Norse believed in, but we don't know a lot about most of them. A lot of the stories are gone, or there are just bits and pieces of them left. If you want to know about every single creature in Norse mythology, there are a lot of books that have more stories about them. You don't have to stop learning about Vikings when you get to the end of this book!

Chapter 6:
Ragnarök

Ragnarok.

We're finally at the chapter about Ragnarök, which is one of the most important stories in Norse mythology. Chapter 2 talked about the beginning of the cosmos in Norse mythology. Ragnarök is about the end.

The Norse didn't believe Ragnarök had already happened. Most of the stories in Norse mythology happened in the past, but Ragnarök is one of the few that hasn't happened yet. The Norse didn't know when it was going to happen, but they knew exactly what would happen. A lot of other cultures have stories about the end of the world, but the Norse version is very detailed. A lot of the gods and creatures you've already learned about come back in Ragnarök.

The word Ragnarök means "Fate of the Gods." It's the story of what happens to the cosmos and the gods when the Norns decide that it's time for the world to end. The Norse believed that since the world started with fire and ice, it will also end with it.

The Beginning of the End

When Ragnarök begins, there will be a long and cold winter. The Earth will be covered in snow and ice just like Niflheim, and the sun will disappear. Humans will go hungry, because no food will grow. Skoll and Hati, two wolves who have been trying to catch the sun and the moon since the beginning of time, will catch Sol and Mani. Skoll and Hati are. After they take these two lights, the stars will also disappear. There will be no more night sky, or even a sky in the daytime. Everything will be pitch black.

Then, at last, Yggdrasil will shake. When Yggdrasil shakes, the mountains will fall, and the monsters that had been locked away from humans will be free. Fenrir will break his chains, and Jormungand will jump out of the ocean in the sky and fall to Earth.

When Fenrir and Jormungand are free, Loki will also be able to break out of his chains. Remember that Loki was locked up after Baldur died. Since he was chained up by the gods, Loki will betray them and command an army of giants. The giants want to destroy the gods and the cosmos. Ragnarök is when they get the chance to do it.

The Gods Go to Battle

From Asgard and Vanaheim, all the gods will see what is happening to the cosmos. They will watch Fenrir eating everything between the land and the sky, while Jormungand spits venom into the water, air, and on the ground. Then, Heimdall will blow his horn, Gjallarhorn. Remember that this horn means there are enemies in Asgard. When the gods look out at the Bifrost bridge, they will see fire giants from the fire world Muspelheim are coming. The gods know Ragnarök will happen someday. They know it will be the end of the world. Even though most of them will die, the gods will still go to battle against the giants.

Odin's Death

Yes, Odin dies in Ragnarök. The god of wisdom who had lived for so long, created the cosmos, and had taken care of the Aesir will meet his end in the last great battle. He doesn't fight alone, though. All the warriors that the Valkyries brought to Valhalla will fight with Odin during Ragnarök. Before they can fight any of the giants, though, Fenrir attacks them. Odin and his warriors will fight as hard as they can, but Fenrir will swallow them whole. After killing Odin, Fenrir will also kill Tyr, the god who tricked him into getting chained up.

One of Odin's sons, Vidar, will see Fenrir eat his father and attack the wolf. Vidar had a special shoe made that would help him fight Fenrir. It is the strongest shoe ever made. With this shoe, Vidar will hold Fenrir's jaws open and stab the wolf, killing it.

Thor's Death

In Ragnarök, Thor will face his old enemy, Jormungand. They will fight a long battle before Thor finally hits Jormungand so many times with his hammer that the serpent dies. During the fight, though, Jormungand will have covered Thor will venom. The venom will poison Thor, and after he kills Jormungand he will die, too.

Freyr's Death

When Odin dies, Freyr will take over the battle. He will go after the leader of the fire giants, Surt. Surt carries a flaming sword he uses to set the world on fire. Freyr and Surt will fight, and in the end, they will kill each other.

SURTUR WITH HIS FLAMING SWORD.

Surt with his flaming sword

Loki's Death

Even the betrayer of the gods, Loki, doesn't escape Ragnarök alive. He and Heimdall had been enemies for a long time. During Ragnarök, they will fight each other until they both die.

The End of the Cosmos

After all the monsters have been slain and the gods and giants have died, there will be nothing left. Every world on Yggdrasil—Asgard, Midgard, Vanaheim, Alfheim, Jotunheim, Niflheim, Muspelheim, Nidavellir, and Hel—will slip into Ginnungagap. This place is the same bottomless pit where the cosmos started. Ginnungagap will be the only thing left when Ragnarök is over.

Why the Norse Believed in Ragnarök

Most stories in mythology teach a lesson. They talk about bravery, why lying is bad, and how to be a better person. Ragnarök is a very different story. It doesn't seem to mean anything. Everyone just dies and the world ends! Why would the Norse people believe in something so sad? Believe it or not, there's a reason why Ragnarök had to happen and why it was important to the Norse.

Life for the Norse and Vikings was hard. They had to fight and work all the time. Just staying alive was a tough thing to do. If you had to live like they did, what would you do? A lot of people might give up. The Norse never did, though.

The gods they believed in were brave, strong, and they didn't quit. Since these were the people the Norse looked up to, it makes sense that they would want to be like the gods. Stories like Ragnarök show that not giving up is important. Even though the gods knew they would all die in Ragnarök, they still fought. They faced their fate.

Since the gods handled death with courage, the Norse knew that they could, too. Life as a human can be scary. It was even scarier in the Viking Age. That's why the Norse came up with stories like Ragnarök. In real life, things end, and people die. They didn't hide this fact in myths. Instead, they let it inspire them to act like the heroes they imagined.

Chapter 7:
Norse Mythology in the Modern World

Even though Norse mythology is 1000 years old, it still influences our world today. The myths are around, of course, but there are a lot of other things we have borrowed from the Norse culture.

Days of the Week

Everyone knows the days of the week: Monday, Tuesday, Wednesday, and so on. Do you know where the names for the days of the week come from, though? Most of them come from the names of the gods. Sunday is named after the goddess of the sun, Sol (Sun's Day). Sol's brother Mani, the god of the moon, has Monday named after him (Moon's Day). Tuesday is Tiw's Day, and Tiw is the Old English name for the god Tyr. If you remember, Tyr is the god of justice and war who had his hand bitten off by Fenrir. Wednesday is Odin's Day, because the name for Odin in Old English is Woden (Woden's Day). Thor's Day is Thursday, and Friday is Frigg's Day (Frigg was Odin's wife). How cool is that? On a Thursday, try wishing someone a happy Thor's Day and see what they say!

English Words

English borrows a lot of words from other languages. Some of our words are even from Old Norse! Think about it: you might be using words that the Vikings used. Some of these words are:

- berserk (Old Norse: berserkr) - means out of control or really mad
- club (Old Norse: klubba) - a club is a blunt weapon
- loan (Old Norse: lán) - means to let someone borrow something
- skill (Old Norse: skil) - something you're good at
- tidings (Old Norse: tíðindi) - news about an event
- give (Old Norse: geffa) - to hand something over to someone else
- take (Old Norse: taka) - opposite of give
- cake (Old Norse: kaka) - the yummy dessert you get on your birthday
- freckles (Old Norse: freknur) - the little dots some people have on their face or bodies
- leg (Old Norse: leggr) - what you use to run and jump
- lad (Old Norse: ladd) - a young man
- anger (Old Norse: angr) - when you're really mad
- happy (Old Norse: happ) - how you feel when you see a birthday cake

Superheroes

You probably know all about Thor the superhero. He's a Marvel Comics character that has also been in movies like *Thor* and *The Avengers*. Stan Lee was the one who decided to use Thor in a comic. He was thinking about what superhero would be stronger than the Hulk, and he couldn't think of anybody. Then he realized that no person could be stronger than the Hulk, but a god could be. Since he had already written about Greek and Roman gods, he decided he wanted to write about Norse gods next.

Thanks to Stan Lee, Marvel Comics, and superhero movies, Norse gods and myths will be around for a very long time.

Conclusion

Even though the Vikings and Norse people have been gone for a long time, the stories they came up with are still important. Who doesn't love tales about Thor fighting giants, Odin leading warriors into battle, and Loki playing tricks? Norse mythology is about a lot more than just gods fighting, though. It tells us what people who lived 1000 years ago believed and how they looked at the world. Without stories like Ragnarök and the many others, we wouldn't know anything about how the Norse thought.

The gods and goddesses in Norse mythology can teach you a lot. Try to be as wise as Odin, as brave as Tyr, as strong as Thor, and loving like Frigg and Freya. When you read about Ragnarök, don't just see it as a story about people going to their doom. Think about why the gods faced their fears instead of running away. Let these stories inspire you, just like they inspired the Vikings.

More from us

Visit our book store at: <u>www.dinobibi.com</u>

History series

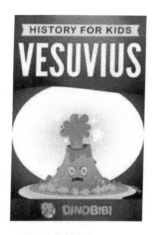

Travel series